Contents

Introduction

Oil and other fossil fuels are among the most important resources on Earth. For centuries they have provided a source of energy for humans, and they continue to fuel modern lifestyles. Their use has been linked to a number of problems, however, including physical damage to the environment and the rise in world temperatures known as global warming. These, and the fact that reserves of fossil fuels are running out, has led governments and other organisations to consider more sustainable – and less damaging – alternatives.

The damaging effect of oil pumps on the landscape is just one of the environmental concerns associated with oil.

Oil and its Uses

Oil is a particularly valuable and versatile resource. It is used as a source of energy, providing heating for homes, schools and offices. Its by-products petrol and diesel are used as a fuel for all types of vehicles, from cars to aeroplanes. Oil is also the raw material used in manufacturing items ranging from plastic bags to medicines and road surfaces. Oil, and all the products that can be made from it, help make our lives easier and more comfortable.

Environmental Issues

There are many obvious benefits of oil, but there are also many problems, most of them linked to environmental damage such as pollution and climate change. The countries where oil is found are often not the ones that use the most. This means that oil has to be transported long distances by land and sea. Accidents such as oil spills are some of the most visible forms of pollution, but it is also important to consider the polluting emissions of the oil tankers themselves. There is also the damage caused to the landscape by drilling for oil. In addition to this, burning oil releases greenhouse gases such as carbon dioxide into the atmosphere and contributes to global warming.

In recent years many efforts have been made to address these issues. Laws have been introduced to make sure that oil is produced, stored and processed in ways that limit environmental damage. New technologies have also helped reduce the problems associated with oil products so that they can be used in less environmentally damaging ways.

Energy Alternatives

One of the most pressing issues is that the world's supplies of oil and other fossil fuels are running

There are over 700 oil refineries worldwide and more are being built. Polluting gases pumped out of these refineries are a major environmental concern.

out. This, more than anything else, has made people consider what alternatives there may be to oil, particularly in terms of energy sources. Methods of harnessing renewable resources such as wind, water and solar power have been successfully developed and are increasingly being used all over the world. These are not simple solutions – many of them have their own problems – but they do offer the possibility of sustainable fuels for the future.

Oil Around the World

Oil (sometimes called petroleum, which means 'rock oil') is one of the most energy-rich fuels available, so it is highly prized. Countries that have large oil reserves have the potential to bring a lot of money into their economies through extracting and selling the oil. However, the processes of drilling for oil and transporting it to refineries to prepare it for use or export can be extremely damaging. The governments of oil-producing countries must consider ways of carrying out these activities that limit the environmental impact.

How Oil is Formed

Like other fossil fuels, oil is formed from the remains of plants and animals that died millions of years ago. As the centuries pass, these remains are gradually buried deep underground, beneath layers of rock and under oceans and seas. When subjected to heat and pressure, the carbon in the plant and animal remains changes into hydrocarbons – the main ingredient of crude oil (oil in its natural, raw form). Natural gas is also formed from hydrocarbons, and builds up in the same places as crude oil. The process by which oil and gas form takes between 300 and 400 million years.

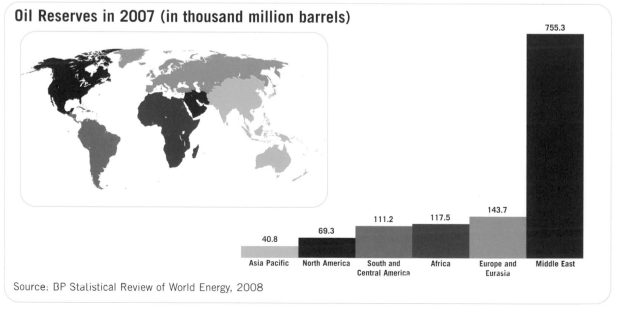

Oil Reserves in 2007 (in thousand million barrels)

Asia Pacific	North America	South and Central America	Africa	Europe and Eurasia	Middle East
40.8	69.3	111.2	117.5	143.7	755.3

Source: BP Statistical Review of World Energy, 2008

This map and chart show the amounts of oil left in different parts of the world. The Middle East leads the way by a huge margin.

Oil storage tanks spread out across the desert in Saudi Arabia – the largest oil-producing country in the world.

Where Oil is Found

Most countries have some oil reserves, but not every country extracts or exports its oil. In some places the amounts are too small to make it worthwhile. In others it is difficult to reach the oil. Sometimes political events affect oil production – wars and global politics can influence the amount of oil that is produced and the countries it is sold to. All this means that the countries with the most reserves are not always the countries that produce and export the most. For example, Canada has nearly as much oil as the United States, but Canada's production is less than half that of the USA. The biggest oil-producing country in the world is Saudi Arabia, followed by Russia, the United States, Iran and China.

There are also differences in the countries that produce the most oil and those that consume, or use, the most. Oil is expensive, so the countries that use most oil are often wealthier nations. The United States uses more oil than any other nation in the world.

The Cost of Oil

The cost of most resources is controlled by the idea of 'supply and demand'. The cost rises if there is not enough of a particular resource to meet the global demand. The price drops if there is more than people need. If prices rise too much, some customers can no longer afford it, so demand falls. In fact this has not happened with oil, as countries have been prepared to pay high prices for this crucial energy resource. However, the prospect of global recession towards the end of 2008 caused dramatic fluctuations in the price of oil.

FACTS IN FOCUS
OPEC

The Organisation of Petroleum Exporting Countries (OPEC) is a group of countries that produce and export oil. The organisation was established in 1960 and its members included several Middle Eastern countries, such as Iran, Iraq, Kuwait and Saudi Arabia, plus others like Venezuela (which has more oil reserves than all of North America put together). More joined later, from all over the world – Indonesia, Libya, the United Arab Emirates (UAE), Algeria, Nigeria, Ecuador, Angola and Gabon. All these are less economically developed countries (LEDCs). There are no European or North American members. OPEC aims to provide a regular supply of oil to countries that import it. It sets the rate at which its member countries can produce oil, and tries to keep prices fair and stable on the world market.

Oil from Underground

To find oil, scientists study rock samples from the earth in a particular area. They can tell from the make-up of the rock whether oil is likely to be present beneath the ground. Once a promising site has been found, a well is drilled and a pump is placed over it. The pump moves up and down, sucking oil up into the well. Sometimes the oil is too thick to flow easily so a second well is drilled. Steam is forced down this well, which pushes the oil up into the first well.

Locating oil is not an exact science and sometimes drilling does not find enough oil to establish a viable oilfield. In places where this occurs, the landscape can be damaged without any benefit. If enough oil is found, many pumps might be placed in the area. The land has to be cleared to make way for the oilfield, and important wildlife habitats can be lost.

New Drilling Technology

Over the past 30 years or so, experts have been finding ways of reducing the environmental effects

A drill rig is used to search for underground oil deposits in Canada.

FACTS IN FOCUS
Oil Shale

Underground reserves are not the only places oil is found. It also exists in surface reserves called oil-shale deposits. Oil shale is a rock made up of a mixture of sand and a substance called kerogen, which contains crude oil. Oil shale can be processed to extract the oil, and there are more reserves of oil shale than there are of crude oil. If ways can be found to address the environmental problems associated with oil shale – including land use for extraction and the emission of greenhouse gases during processing – oil shale might be the solution to the world's declining crude-oil supplies.

of drilling for oil. Satellites and other technologies have made it easier to locate oil without drilling. New techniques also mean that oil from a single well can be pumped from a larger area, so fewer wells are needed. This technology is expensive so only wealthier countries can afford to use it, but there are increasing demands for it to be made available in other countries too, so that the impact on the landscape can be reduced. In addition to this, laws have been introduced stating that when all the oil has been pumped from a well, it must be filled in, or 'plugged', rather than just left as it is. In this way, the landscape can slowly recover.

Oil from Beneath the Sea

Large amounts of oil are found under the sea. A platform, or 'rig', is built over the area where oil has been found. These platforms can either be fixed or floating. Wells are sunk into the ocean floor; the oil and gas are then pumped up and stored. Undersea drilling is often more difficult than drilling on land because of the extra pressure put on equipment by the force of the water. This increases the risk of breakdown and spills. If oil gets into the water it can harm marine ecosystems. There is also a risk to the people who work on oil rigs – the structures can collapse or fires can break out.

Worker safety is now of primary concern. Where once employees lived and worked on the same platform, there are now separate rigs like floating hotels. A safety boat is kept near the platform at all times to help evacuate in an emergency.

The environmental impacts of undersea drilling, such as leaks and disturbance to marine life, are more difficult to limit, but organisations are looking at new drilling techniques to help. It is now possible to run drills horizontally from the coast out to sea, which means that rigs are not needed.

CASE STUDY

Gulf of Mexico: Undersea Ecosystems

Offshore oil platforms can actually be helpful to marine wildlife. The legs of the platform act like an artificial reef. Creatures such as spiny oysters, barnacles, sponges and corals attach themselves to the legs, establishing an ecosystem. Larger creatures are then attracted to the area – fish, sea turtles, sharks and sea urchins. The oil rig offers them shelter as well as food. One of the most notable examples of where this has occurred is the Gulf of Mexico, which has some of the largest oil rigs in the world. 'Rig diving' has become popular here, as divers come to experience this spectacular underwater world.

'Rig-to-reef' programmes have been established in a number of areas and are a popular diving experience.

Transporting Oil

Once oil has been extracted from beneath the ground, it has to be transported to refineries for processing. Because oil reserves are often situated in remote areas, the oil has to travel long distances to reach the refineries. Transporting oil usually takes place via tankers or pipelines. Both these methods involve environmental risks. So what are these risks and what is being done to prevent them?

Tankers

The spilling of oil during transportation is one of the greatest risks associated with oil. If oil tankers get into difficulties at sea, the oil can pollute marine environments. Accidents have damaged ecosystems in places like the West Indies (*Atlantic Empress*, 1979), Alaska (*Exxon Valdez*, 1989) and Spain (*Prestige*, 2002). Oil spills at sea usually have a more damaging impact than those on land because oil floats on water and spreads over huge areas, coating coastlines with a film of oil. If oil gets on seabirds' feathers they cannot fly, and their food supply of fish is poisoned. Shellfish and smaller creatures die and it can take a long time for populations to grow again. The livelihoods of local people, particularly fishermen, can be threatened.

Over the past 20 years, the frequency of oil spills has reduced, although they still occur. This is partly because greater care has been taken when preparing oil tankers. The European Union has passed laws banning oil being transported in single-hull tankers and putting a limit on the age of the ships that can be used. Groups like Greenpeace campaign vigorously against the transportation of oil by tanker, and have drawn global attention to the environmental problems it can cause.

Pipelines

There is less risk of oil spills with pipelines, but there are still problems. Areas of land must be cleared to make way for pipelines, which destroys wildlife habitats. Pipelines cannot be placed underground for long distances, so the longer ones are built on stilts. This at least means that animals can move beneath them and their path to finding

The oil tanker *Prestige* splits in half off the coast of Spain, spilling 70,000 tonnes of oil into the sea.

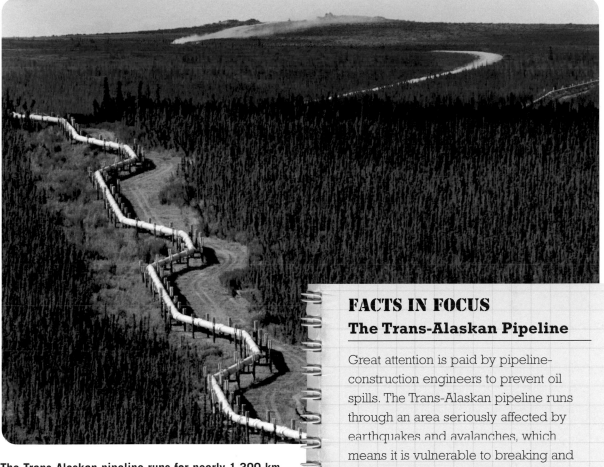

The Trans-Alaskan pipeline runs for nearly 1,300 km from northern Alaska to a sea port in the south.

food and shelter is not blocked. Underground pipes can affect fragile environments such as the frozen tundra of Alaska. They can also pose a threat to humans. Nigeria is a major oil producer and has many underground pipelines, some of which cut through urban areas. In May 2008 a bulldozer accidentally hit one of these oil pipes, causing a huge explosion. More than 100 people were killed.

EXPERT VIEW

'Our town lives on fishing and tourism. If more incidents like this or worse occur it is the economic future of the town that is threatened.'
GREGOIRE MBA MBA, MAYOR OF KRIBI IN CAMEROON,
AFTER AN OIL-PIPELINE LEAK MADE 500 PEOPLE HOMELESS

FACTS IN FOCUS
The Trans-Alaskan Pipeline

Great attention is paid by pipeline-construction engineers to prevent oil spills. The Trans-Alaskan pipeline runs through an area seriously affected by earthquakes and avalanches, which means it is vulnerable to breaking and allowing oil to spill out. This pipeline has built-in systems to stop it breaking. The stilts allow the pipeline to move sideways, so it stays intact if hit by snowfall in an avalanche. The line is also built in a zigzag pattern, which strengthens it against earthquakes.

Pipelines are the most cost-effective way of transporting oil over long distances and they have a greater safety record than any other way of transporting oil, but they still carry risks. However, steps can be taken to ensure their damaging effects are limited. Regular checks can be made to make sure the pipes are working properly and are not corroded. When new pipelines are planned they are now subject to careful safety and environmental standards.

Refining Oil

Once oil reaches the refinery, it is processed to extract all its useful parts. These are then made into a wide variety of products. The refining process uses large amounts of energy and, like a lot of industrial activity, it releases polluting gases into the atmosphere. However, steps are being taken to ensure that oil processing and the manufacture of oil products are carried out in a more sustainable way.

Hydrocarbons – the Raw Material

The most useful thing about crude oil is that it is packed with hydrocarbons, which are full of energy. At the refinery, a process called distillation separates out these hydrocarbons based on their boiling points. Gas has the lowest boiling point. Once they have been separated out, the different substances can be processed further into the useful products that we use every day – from the petrol or diesel used to power our cars to the bitumen (or tar) that surfaces the roads we drive on.

Storage Problems and Solutions

A vast amount of crude oil arrives at refineries, and it must be stored somewhere. The oil is kept

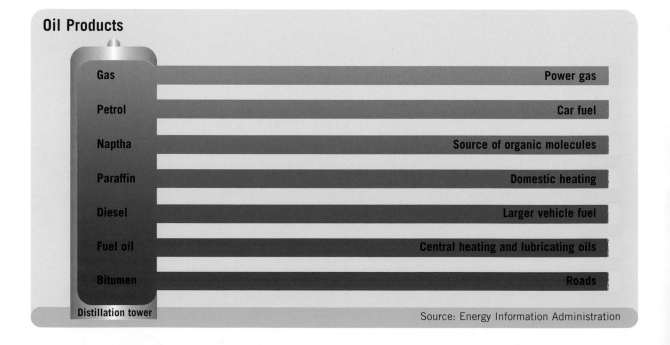

Oil Products

Gas	Power gas
Petrol	Car fuel
Naptha	Source of organic molecules
Paraffin	Domestic heating
Diesel	Larger vehicle fuel
Fuel oil	Central heating and lubricating oils
Bitumen	Roads

Distillation tower

Source: Energy Information Administration

in large tanks, often buried underground, until it is ready to be refined. When processed, the products must also be stored until they can be further processed or transported. There have been many cases of oil and its products leaking from these storage tanks and causing pollution. A big concern is when leaked oil gets into local water supplies and contaminates drinking water. In the United States, after a petrol ingredient called methyl tertiary butyl ether (MTBE) affected drinking water, its use was banned in the refining process.

Recent laws in MEDCs, including the United States, have required that all underground storage tanks are replaced by new ones that have a double lining to reduce the risk of leakage. This will be a long and costly process to implement, but ultimately it will significantly reduce the pollution to soil and water from underground oil leaks.

A distillation tower at an oil refinery in New Zealand. The different hydrocarbon products are piped out of the tower into underground storage tanks.

FACTS IN FOCUS
The World's Largest Oil Refineries

Refinery	Country	Barrels per day
Paraguana	Venezuela	940,000
SK Energy	South Korea	817,000
Reliance Industries	India	661,000
GS Caltex	South Korea	650,000
ExxonMobil	Singapore	605,000
ExxonMobil	United States (Texas City)	557,000
S-Oil	South Korea	520,000
Hovensa LLC	Virgin Islands (Caribbean)	495,000
ExxonMobil	United States (Baton Rouge)	493,500
Mina al-Ahmadi	Kuwait	470,000

Source: Oil and Gas Journal

Often situated near water supplies, refineries like this one in South Africa can cause problems such as chemical leaks and air pollution.

Air Pollution

Air pollution is one of the greatest concerns about oil refineries. Some of them pump out more than 100 different pollutants into the atmosphere every day. These include substances like lead, which can affect the health of people living nearby – causing anything from skin irritations to cancer – and polluting gases like carbon dioxide and methane that contribute to global warming.

In South Africa, for example, there are five oil refineries, which emit dangerous levels of polluting gases. A recent report suggested that children at a school near an oil refinery in Durban suffered between 30 and 40 per cent more respiratory problems than those living further away, because of the emissions from the refinery. Environmental Justice Action in South Africa, an environmental group, is campaigning to draw attention to the effects on people and the environment. As well as noting the levels of air pollutants, they have found harmful waste dumped on the land and water pollution from chemical discharges. Accidental spills are not uncommon. This group encourages concerned individuals to support its campaign by talking to their local politicians.

Controlling Pollution

In more economically developed countries (MEDCs), oil processing and storage are controlled by government standards. Inspections are regularly carried out to prevent air, water and ground pollution. Pollution controls are improved as often as possible. In the early twenty-first century, pollution levels were a quarter of what they were in the late 1970s. In LEDCs such as China, however, the situation is more of a problem. In April 2008, China was officially recognised as the most polluting country on the planet, and energy processing is a large part of this problem. The country is industrialising rapidly, and controlling this growth in a sustainable way is difficult.

Engineers inspect the pipes at a refinery near Budapest in Hungary. Leak prevention and environmental controls are strictly enforced in MEDCs.

Individuals already recognise the problems of pollution caused by refineries and try to draw government attention to it. In May 2008 a demonstration was held in Chengdu in south-west China to protest against the building of an oil refinery near the city. The development of such industry cannot be prevented, but it is important that countries with the experience and technology to move the oil industry forward in a sustainable way work together with countries like China to make sure that environmental impacts are reduced.

EXPERT VIEW

'Nearly one in three Americans lives within 30 miles of a refinery. This … subjects the public to increased cancer risks and other chronic health hazards. Oil companies have the technology and the resources to fix this problem.'
JOHN WALKE, CLEAR AIR PROGRAM, UNITED STATES

CASE STUDY

United States: Toledo Refinery

In 1997, BP's oil refinery at Toledo, Ohio, installed devices called 'flare flow meters'. These burn the gases created by hydrocarbons before they are released into the atmosphere. Since they were installed, the flare flow meters have reduced emissions of carbon dioxide and other polluting gases from the Toledo refinery by around 5,000 tonnes a year. The BP oil company was awarded the Governor's Award for Outstanding Achievement in Pollution Prevention in 1998. The success of the flare flow meters has made other oil companies consider the environmental impacts of the refining process, and has been a big advance in making oil refining more sustainable.

An oil refinery in Beijing, China, pumps polluting gases into the atmosphere. These hang as smog over the area, affecting people's health and the environment.

Plastic Production

'Plastic' is a single word referring to a huge range of different materials. What most have in common is that they are made from petroleum. Plastics are malleable, which means they can be bent or shaped into objects or made into fabrics. Their versatility means we are using more plastic products than ever before. But as well as using a valuable fossil fuel as their raw material, there are other problems with plastics.

How is Plastic Made?

Like other oil products, plastic comes from the hydrocarbons found in crude oil. Plastic polymers are made up of long chains of heavier hydrocarbons – the ones that do not make efficient fuels. To make a plastic product, the polymers are heated until they become soft.

Plastic products are all around us – in everything from house guttering to food packaging.

FACTS IN FOCUS
Plastic Polymers

Polymers are long chains of hydrocarbon molecules, the building blocks of plastics. Although many polymers are man-made from the by-products of crude oil, some occur naturally – cotton, linen and natural rubber are all polymers. It is the structure of polymers that makes plastic tough yet malleable: the long chains are tangled up like spaghetti, but they can be separated by heating. When heated, the chains move apart and can be moulded into new positions. When they cool down, they keep these strong structures.

A worker prepares a plastic resin in an injection mould in a factory in Singapore.

This molten substance is then injected into a mould in the shape of the product. There it cools and hardens into the shape of the mould. This is called 'injection moulding', and items like toys and car parts are made in this way.

Objects like plastic bottles are made in a process called 'blow moulding', in which molten plastic is poured into a mould and then air is blown into it. This inflates the material to fill the mould.

The Benefits of Plastics

Plastics have become part of our everyday lives. We use them in all sorts of ways, from packaging such as bags and bottles to toys and household goods like refrigerators. Plastic products such as polyester and nylon are even used to make clothing. They are cheap to make, tough, flexible and waterproof. Plastic molecules can act like

fibres, so they can be made into products that might previously have relied on natural materials such as wood or paper. This saves on precious natural resources like trees.

In fact, plastics are quite energy efficient. For example, making plastic bags can use up to 40 per cent less energy than making paper bags, and because they are lighter, they can be packed up and transported more efficiently.

The big drawbacks of plastics are the amount of fossil fuels used to make them – in both the raw material and for powering the factories where the products are made – and the fact that they are generally not biodegradable (they take a long time to decompose after they have been thrown away). There is also a large littering problem with items such as plastic bags. So, what can be done to reduce the impact of plastics on the environment?

Landfill Sites

If plastic is just thrown away rather than being recycled, it will end up in landfill. There it will stay for thousands of years because it takes so long to break down. To reduce the amount of plastic going into landfill, some countries export it overseas, where it can be recycled and reused. For example, the United States sends some of its plastic waste to Indonesia and Hong Kong. This reduces the amount of plastic going to landfill in the USA, and the importing countries can use the recycled plastic as a cheap raw material. It provides income for people in LEDCs. However, in some cases the plastic cannot be recycled, so the receiving country has to dispose of it in landfill. In this situation the problem has simply been transferred from one country to another.

Biodegradable Plastic

The reason that normal plastics do not decompose quickly is because their long polymer molecules are too large and tightly bound together to be easily broken apart. Scientists have been trying to solve this problem by developing plastics from natural polymers rather than man-made ones. Plastics made from plant materials are more easily decomposed by micro-organisms – these biodegradable types are 'digested' by natural organisms in the earth. This reduces litter, landfill and impact on wildlife. The downside to biodegradable plastic is that in the process of decomposing, carbon dioxide is produced – a greenhouse gas that is released into the atmosphere and contributes to global warming.

Recycling Plastic

Recycling is the best way of reducing plastic pollution. Recycling programmes are common in many countries, for plastics and other materials that can be reused. In some European countries, such as Germany, people even have to pay for the disposal of anything that is not recycled. Recyclable plastics are collected in huge skips at refuse-collection points and taken for sorting at

Men work at a landfill site in Indonesia. Countries in this part of the world import plastic waste from other nations to reuse, but not all plastic can be recycled so some of it ends up in sites like this.

This machine in a factory in the United States is 'growing' biodegradable plastic from bacteria.

recycling depots. Most sorting is done by hand. There are different types of plastic and they are recycled in different ways, so they must be sorted into their types, as well as by colour.

Technology is being introduced to sort plastics automatically, using methods such as X-ray fluorescence and infrared spectroscopy. These systems will be quicker, cheaper and more accurate than identifying the plastics manually. Once sorted, plastic is melted down and re-shaped into new objects, or it is mechanically shredded into tiny pieces for transport elsewhere to make new things.

EXPERT VIEW

'The challenge in developing biodegradable plastics is creating a product as good as, if not better than, its petroleum counterpart. The industry is looking for a versatile product that can be used for multiple markets.'
JUSTIN BARONE, PROFESSOR OF BIOLOGICAL SYSTEMS ENGINEERING AT VIRGINIA TECH UNIVERSITY, USA

FACTS IN FOCUS
Why Aren't We Recycling More?

At the moment, only a small percentage of plastic waste is recycled when compared to other materials like paper and metals. Part of the reason for this is that recycling plastic is more complicated than recycling other items. There are different types of plastic and many places only recycle some of them. Consumers do not always understand what can be recycled and what can't. Another reason is cost. Recycled plastic is more expensive than new plastic, so companies choose new plastic for their packaging. If people were willing to pay a little more for recycled plastic items, it could make a big difference to the amount of plastic waste being created.

Plastic packaging such as plastic bottles often has a number code that shows how it should be separated for recycling.

Burning Plastic

Burning, or incinerating, some types of plastic can release poisonous chemicals into the air, but this does not mean that burning plastic as a means of disposal is out of the question. In fact, there is a big advantage to burning plastic waste. Like most materials made out of fossil fuels, plastics contain a lot of energy – the same as petrol or gas. The heat energy released when plastic is burned can be harnessed and used. Waste-to-energy plants are power plants that incinerate plastic and other waste and turn the energy released into electricity. There are 90 of these plants in the United States alone, providing electricity for three million homes.

Burning plastics is not a cheap method of generating electricity – it costs more than using coal or some forms of renewable power such as water or nuclear energy – but it can significantly reduce the amount of waste that ends up in landfill, and has the potential to be a good, sustainable method of reducing plastic pollution.

Plastic Pollution in the Oceans

Sixty million tonnes of plastic are produced every year around the world. Some is recycled and re-used, but a lot finds its way into the sea. Our oceans contain millions of tonnes of plastic. Some breaks down into microscopic pieces, known as 'mermaids' tears', giving the impression that it has gone away – but it has not. Pollutants in the oceans stick to these tiny pieces. Small enough to be eaten by creatures at the bottom of the food chain, these poisons are passed on to much larger creatures, including humans.

Waste left on a beach is likely to find its way into the ocean, polluting our waters.

CASE STUDY

Pacific Ocean: Crisis on Midway

The remote island of Midway in the northern Pacific Ocean, part of Hawaii, 1,600 km north-west of Honolulu, is an example of how plastic pollution in the oceans can have a damaging effect. Ocean currents concentrate a mass of floating plastic here and much is in the sea surrounding this uninhabited island, coming ashore on to the beaches. The main residents of Midway are albatrosses. They breed here, but the death rate among young birds is tragically high, because of plastic poisoning and choking. Pieces of plastic become wedged in the bird's mouth or gullet, preventing it from eating and leading to a slow death from starvation.

The albatrosses on the island of Midway are under threat from the high levels of plastic pollution on the shores and in the surrounding waters.

Even if we were to put no more plastic into the oceans at all, it would still take thousands of years to overcome this crisis because it will take so long for what is already there to break down. Some of the plastic waste in the oceans is a result of carelessness by individuals, who do not dispose of plastic waste properly on beaches, for example. Ships also dump a lot of plastic waste overboard to get rid of it.

Organisations like the environmental charity Greenpeace are campaigning not only for people to be more aware of what happens to their plastic waste, but also for clean-up operations in our seas. Laws such as the Marine Plastic Pollution Research and Control Act in the United States now make the dumping of plastic waste in the oceans illegal.

TAKE ACTION

Preserving the environment from plastic pollution can start with individuals. Re-using and recycling plastic materials is key to a sustainable future for the plastics industry.

- Buy a re-usable drinks bottle and refill it as necessary.
- Re-use your shopping bags rather than taking new ones every time you go to the supermarket.
- Buy food products that come in biodegradable packaging – these are 100 per cent sustainable.
- Buy drinks that have photodegradable plastic ring pulls (which break down in light). These have been available since the 1990s.

Gas from the Ground

Oil and natural gas are usually found together. Because gas is lighter, it collects over the liquid oil in the same trap. When people first began drilling for oil, they could not see a use for gas, so they just burned it off – wasting it completely. Today, the gas is piped off and used as an energy source in its own right.

Finding and Drilling for Gas

Estimates vary about how much natural gas there is left beneath the surface of our planet. Although many new reserves were discovered late in the twentieth century, just like with oil some gas fields are more expensive to tap into than others, so gas prices around the world influence whether or not it is worth drilling for gas. Despite this, reserves of natural gas will probably last until around 2085 – longer than our oil reserves.

The process of locating gas and oil deposits has been transformed by the invention of advanced technology. Scientists use seismic waves to map underground rock structures three-dimensionally. The waves are projected into the ground. They behave differently according to the density and structure of the rock. This is rather like bouncing a ball on different surfaces – the characteristics of the bounce vary from one surface to another. Some of the waves are reflected back to give a detailed picture of local geology.

Test drills are carried out to see whether gas and oil are trapped. It is not necessary to pump up the gas the way oil has to be brought to the surface – as soon as drilling begins, gas rushes to the surface to release the pressure it is under. However, it is important to control the flow of the gas to make sure none of it is lost.

Uses of Natural Gas

Natural gas is much cleaner and greener than oil or coal. When burnt, it releases fewer polluting gases and almost no particle waste. Although reserves are limited, and natural gas is not a sustainable resource, its benefits mean it is being used more and more in a number of ways.

Power Generation

Gas can be burned to create steam. This is used to power turbines that generate electricity, or gas is used directly in a gas turbine for the same purpose. It is one of the cleanest methods of generating power from fossil fuels – natural gas produces less carbon

A bus powered by natural gas in Sweden. Natural-gas vehicles are far better for the environment than those powered by oil products such as petrol or diesel.

dioxide per unit of electricity made than other sources. Its potential for the future is promising, since gas supplies are likely to last longer than oil.

Domestic Use

Although it is rapidly becoming more expensive, gas as a fuel for heating and cooking remains cheaper than electricity. Gas tumble dryers are becoming more popular because they cost one-third of those powered by electricity. New-style condensing central-heating boilers that can be gas-powered are far more efficient than previous designs. Much smaller, they can be fitted into the space of an ordinary kitchen cupboard.

Natural-Gas Transport

Natural gas is a cleaner transport fuel than either petrol or diesel. In 2005, the countries using the largest numbers of gas vehicles were Argentina, Brazil, Pakistan, Italy, Iran and the United States. LNG (liquefied natural gas), made of a mixture of propane and butane, is another gas vehicle fuel, but LNG and natural gas cannot be used in the same engine. Natural gas is also used as a fuel for aircraft.

A seismic survey team drills down to survey the land for gas and oil deposits in Pakistan.

CASE STUDY

Russia: Gas-Powered Aircraft

Tupolev, a Russian aircraft manufacturer, is developing LNG and hydrogen-powered aircraft engines for both passenger and freight planes. These fuel sources are much more environmentally friendly than oil-based fuels, not just because oil reserves are in serious decline, but because the polluting emissions of such craft are much lower when powered by gas. Commercial flights on LNG or hydrogen-powered aircraft are not likely to be available for some time because of the high cost of liquid hydrogen. When it happens, though, it is still anticipated that the cost of flights will be up to 40 per cent less than in traditional aircraft because of the rising cost of oil-based fuels.

Gas is stored in enormous tanks. They rise and fall as they are filled and emptied.

Landscape and Climate Problems

Burning natural gas does release greenhouse gases such as carbon dioxide and methane (the gas it is mostly made up of) into the atmosphere, contributing to global warming. However, it emits far lower levels of polluting gases than burning coal or oil. There are other benefits too. Natural gas creates fewer waste products that can pollute water supplies, for example.

Just as with oil, there are also environmental problems with obtaining, transporting and storing natural gas. But, as with oil, more sustainable solutions are being introduced. Drilling for gas damages land and marine environments, but new technologies mean that the damage is far less widespread than it used to be. The fact that oil and gas are largely found in the same places means two resources can be tapped at the same time. Although gas leaks in storage facilities can cause dangerous explosions, gas-storage facilities actually have good safety records thanks to careful monitoring of tanks and equipment.

Transporting Gas

Most gas transported across land goes by pipeline. There are both advantages and disadvantages to this. Although pipelines are expensive to build, they are relatively cheap to operate. The big disadvantage is that gas is low-density, so not much energy is transported at a time, compared with piping oil, for example.

When gas needs to be transported long distances across oceans, special ships are used, called LNG carriers. These are designed to carry liquefied natural gas. Road tankers travel short distances, usually within a country. Here, the gas is compressed rather than liquefied (CNG). Across most of North America, Russia and the countries of the European Union, most households use gas, so pipes (mains) must be laid and maintained to deliver this essential fuel. The World Bank has set up emission limits for natural-gas use, which ensures that the resource is controlled.

A gas main is laid in the United Kingdom. Pipeline networks like this are an essential part of supplying households with an increasingly used power source.

CASE STUDY

Finland: Clean Gas

Natural gas has been used in Finland for more than 30 years. Because it is safe, clean and competitive in price, demand is increasing, both for home and industrial energy. A 35 per cent increase in use is expected between 2005 and 2015. 'Expansion 2010' is a project to expand and improve the gas-transmission system. Some industries are switching to gas from other energy sources because of its environmental and economic advantages. This expansion in natural-gas use has significantly reduced Finland's energy emissions because it has replaced more polluting forms of energy like coal and oil. For this reason, gas is playing an important part Finland's programme to reduce climate change.

Oil as a Fuel

The use of oil we are most familiar with is as a source of fuel, particularly in the form of petrol and diesel to power our vehicles. The emissions caused by the burning of oil for energy is a great cause of concern to governments, environmentalists and indeed individuals all over the world, because of the effect it has on our climate.

Fuels from Crude Oil

A 160-litre barrel of crude oil can produce up to 167 litres of petroleum products, around 100 litres of which are petrol and diesel. Petrol, or gasoline, is used as a fuel in cars and smaller vans. Diesel is increasingly used in cars because, although more expensive per litre, it is more efficient than petrol, so it is slightly more environmentally friendly. Kerosene is mainly used as an aviation fuel – for powering aircraft.

Kerosene can also be used for heating homes and is most useful in countries with remote

Kerosene is shared out among survivors of the tsunami in Banda Aceh, Indonesia. Kerosene is used as a fuel in remote areas and where the infrastructure of other power supplies is unavailable.

CASE STUDY

Vietnam: Energy Issues

Compared to many other countries, Vietnam produces and uses very little energy. In recent years there has been a greater demand to improve the energy industry, as the population grows, and people want a better standard of living. Vietnam actually has more oil reserves than some other Asian Pacific countries, including Australia, but it currently has very little in the way of processing facilities. In 2005 construction began on the first oil refinery in Vietnam, bringing the country closer to self-sufficiency. The Dung Quat refinery will make millions of tonnes of important oil products such as petrol, diesel and kerosene available to the Vietnamese.

The Dung Quat refinery in Vietnam will greatly improve the country's energy situation.

regions, where people cannot access natural gas for heating and cooking. Canada, the United States, Australia and New Zealand are examples of MEDCs that make use of kerosene as a heating fuel. In India, kerosene is an important cooking fuel. The government subsidises this, so that even the poorest families can afford it.

Environmental Impact of Oil Fuels

The big issue surrounding all these fuels is the gases they release into the atmosphere when burned in vehicle engines. The worst of these is carbon dioxide, which is a factor in global warming. Greenhouse gases like carbon dioxide are present in the atmosphere, and play an important role. They allow sunlight to enter the atmosphere and then they trap some of the heat there as it bounces back off the Earth. As human activity like burning oil products creates more greenhouse gases, though, too much heat gets trapped in the atmosphere, causing global temperatures to rise. This is why governments all over the world are trying to reduce their greenhouse-gas emissions.

EXPERT VIEW

'To build cars, you need a lot of power… One of the things we're trying to do is continue to build quality vehicles while lessening the impact on the environment. This system we put into place is ecologically sound. It's a clean-burning fuel and makes a perfect power source for the plant's boilers. It's reduced our dependence on coal.'

MICHAEL SCHAFRAN, GENERAL MOTORS, ON THE LAUNCH OF A PROJECT TO USE LANDFILL GAS AS A FUEL

What are the Alternatives?

Scientists have been working towards changing the composition of petrol and diesel so that they do not release so many gases. These new fuels are called 'reformulated fuels' and they are becoming more widely used as people realise how damaging normal petrol and diesel can be. Although reformulated fuels can reduce the emissions from vehicles, they are still oil-based, so they do not address the problem of the dwindling supply of fossil fuels, or the environmental problems linked with extracting and refining oil. However, there are alternatives that do not use fossil fuels at all. These are known as biofuels.

Biofuels

Like fossil fuels, biofuels come from decaying organic matter. Unlike fossil fuels, though, the organic matter – usually plants – in biofuels has only recently died. This might not sound like a big difference, but biofuel sources, which are often grown especially for the purpose, have already removed carbon dioxide from the air, so they are what scientists call 'carbon neutral'. Fossil fuels release carbon dioxide that has been buried for millions of years. Biofuels include biogas, biodiesel and bioethanol. Biofuels are being used more and more in the countries of Europe, Asia and North and South America.

These fuel pumps in California offer a range of biofuels, including biodiesel and ethanol.

FACTS IN FOCUS
Adopting Biofuels

An increasing number of LEDCs are using biofuels. In China, 16 per cent of all cars now run on biofuel. Since 2007, Thailand has used a mixture of ethanol from palm oil with petrol, reducing the oil products needed for fuel, and Malaysia and Indonesia are following Thailand's lead. Colombia uses a similar fuel in its larger cities. Some MEDCs have also set biofuel targets. The United Kingdom started adding 2.5 per cent of biofuel to its petrol in April 2008 and has plans to increase this. Canada aims to make just under half of its vehicle fuel 10 per cent ethanol by the year 2010.

Biogas is essentially methane (the main ingredient of natural gas). One of the most potent greenhouse gases, it is given off by rotting waste on landfill sites. It can be harnessed for burning as a fuel. Biogas 'digesters' (machines that can help convert waste into biogas) are becoming more common on farms, particularly in MEDCs, where the gas is given off when crop and animal wastes decompose under controlled conditions. A similar process is also used in parts of Africa and Asia to make gas for cooking or to power engines.

Biomass

The decaying matter that produces the different biofuels is known as biomass. Biomass can be wild plants, crops that are grown especially for the purpose, or food-crop waste, but it can be animal waste too. In poorer parts of the world, people have been using biomass for centuries and it is still the most common everyday energy resource.

MEDCs have jumped on the bandwagon to produce biomass energy crops in an effort to

A farmer in Switzerland fills his tractor tank with liquid manure. This can be turned into biogas to create electricity.

reduce the environmental effects of using oil. However, there are negative consequences to using biomass. As land is given over to growing crops for biomass energy, there is less land available for growing food crops. This has pushed global food prices much higher and can hurt the poor of the world. In the Amazon rainforest, large areas are being cleared to grow soya beans for biofuels. This is destroying an extremely valuable natural resource, and cancelling out any benefits of the end product.

One possible solution to this might be to make better use of biofuels from waste materials. Some Scandinavian countries already get between 10 and 15 per cent of their national energy from wood waste generated by the pulp and paper industries. With so much waste being put into landfill all over the world, more could be done to harness the natural emissions created by this waste and put it to good use. The sensible use of waste material in this way benefits everyone.

Natural Power

The declining reserves of fossil fuels like oil have led to great developments in alternative power sources. These are known as renewable resources, and they include wind, water, solar and geothermal power – all of which can be harnessed and used for electricity generation and to meet other energy needs. Although they are hailed as the solution to the power crisis the world is facing, there are many factors to consider if these solutions are to be developed sustainably.

At this solar power plant outside Seville in southern Spain, more than 600 mirrors reflect and focus the Sun's rays to turn water into steam. The steam is then blasted into turbines to generate power.

EXPERT VIEW

'For a country like Saudi Arabia … one of the most important sources of energy to look at and to develop is solar energy. One of the research efforts that we are going to undertake is to see how we make Saudi Arabia a centre for solar energy research and hopefully over the next 30 to 50 years we will be a major megawatt exporter. In the same way we are an oil exporter, we can also be an exporter of power.'

ALI AL-NUAIMI, SAUDI OIL MINISTER

Solar Power

There are two ways in which the Sun's energy can be converted into usable electricity. Photovoltaic (PV) cells change sunlight directly into electricity. We already use many devices that have this technology built in, including watches, calculators and illuminated road signs. Such devices are especially useful in remote places because they do not have to be connected to an electricity-grid system in order to work. In solar power plants, special panels collect the Sun's energy and use it to heat water into steam, which then powers a generator to create electricity.

Solar energy is renewable, limitless, free (once the stations are set up) and non-polluting, so what are the problems? The main one is its unreliability – it is not very efficient in places where it is often cloudy – or at night! However, solar power has huge potential for remote tropical villages. In the Sahel region of Africa (a semi-desert zone just south of the Sahara) fuel wood is limited, yet the Sun's heat is plentiful. Simple inventions, like a solar cooker, could solve the energy problem in such regions.

Wind Power

The wind is harnessed and turned into usable energy by wind turbines. These are similar to old-fashioned windmills. The wind turns blades that are connected to a drive shaft. The drive shaft turns an electric generator, creating electricity. Collections of wind turbines grouped together are called a wind farm. They can be as small as two or three turbines, often found on farms in Europe, or hundreds. The Horse Hollow Wind Energy Center in Texas, with 421 turbines, was the largest in the world when it was built, but there are plans for larger ones. Most wind farms are independent power producers, privately owned so not belonging to public utility companies. Farms generate their own power and sell any spare to the national grid. Everyone gains.

The main difficulty with wind-power generation is that it does not work when there is no wind. Careful location of wind farms can largely overcome this problem. On the coast there is often very little shelter, and out at sea there is no shelter at all, so winds blow freely, and many plans for wind farms propose to establish them out at sea.

CASE STUDY

United Kingdom: The London Array

The United Kingdom sees a future in offshore wind farms and plans to build the world's largest offshore wind farm (341 turbines) in the Thames Estuary. Called the London Array, it will cost £1.5 billion and provide one per cent of the country's electricity needs. This will stop 1.9 million tonnes of carbon dioxide entering the atmosphere from more polluting forms of energy generation. Some people think the London Array will lie too close to shipping lanes and could disturb ships' radar. Bird habitats could also be at risk, although 175 turbines will be built first to measure any impact before the second phase is begun. The project has already been altered to protect a rare bird, the red-throated diver.

There are few environmental problems with wind power. The most serious is the impact on wild birds, which can fly into the blades of the turbines. The noise pollution from wind farms is also becoming a problem. Some people think that wind farms ruin the landscape, but others think they look elegant, or are at least preferable to traditional power plants.

An offshore wind farm in Denmark. The country is the world leader in wind power – 20 per cent of its electricity comes from this source.

The Itaipu dam, on the Paraná river between Paraguay and Brazil, supplies 93 per cent of Paraguay's and 20 per cent of Brazil's energy needs, and has been called one of the Seven Wonders of the Modern World.

Hydroelectric Power

Hydroelectricity, often called HEP, is the most widely used form of renewable energy. HEP generation requires fast-flowing water from reliable heavy rainfall throughout the year. Waterfalls are used in Iceland and Norway. In places where there is less rainfall or running water, dams are built to trap and store the water.

The problems with hydroelectricity come with the building of dams and reservoirs. Vast areas of land are needed, so vegetation is cleared, valuable habitats are lost, and settlements have to be moved. Villagers were moved away from the River Volta in West Africa for the Volta Dam Project, for example. People found themselves living away from a clean, reliable water source and from their traditional ancestral lands. Once hydroelectric schemes are operating there are other problems. Rotting vegetation underwater can spoil water quality and release methane gas, and dams can collapse, causing

disastrous flooding. Careful planning can limit the environmental impacts, and hydroelectricity remains one of the more sustainable solutions to the energy crisis, particularly in LEDCs.

Tidal Power

Tides are one of the most reliable and predictable renewable-energy resources. Although tidal barrages used to harness tidal energy are expensive to build and maintain, over time the power produced is nevertheless good value. Suitable sites are limited, though, and negative environmental effects occur. When a barrage is in place, salt water does not penetrate as far up the estuary. The water behind the barrage is fresher, damaging saltwater habitats for birds. Ecosystems are also affected by a build-up of sediments, which are not washed out to sea so efficiently. Sluices (gaps) in the barrage are built to allow fish through safely, but that does not prevent them trying to swim through the turbines. Fifteen per cent of fish passing through are lost.

Wave Power

The movement of waves can also be used to generate electricity in wave power stations. The best locations for wave farms are places with strong westerly winds – the United States, Western Europe, Japan and New Zealand are ideal. Norway began conducting experiments in wave power in the early 1990s but was unsuccessful. At the end of 2007, the Pacific Gas and Electric Company announced plans for the first American commercial wave power plant, to be located off the North Californian coast. Japan has an active wave-energy development plan. Experiments to focus waves to increase their size and concentrate energy to turn turbines have had some success, and small

developments are planned to power isolated coastal communities. Wave power does little damage and is certainly a resource worth developing.

FACTS IN FOCUS
Ocean Thermal Energy Conversion

Insolation (the Sun's energy) heats ocean surface water. If the temperature difference between the warm surface water and the colder deeper water is at least 25°C, as can happen in tropical regions, it can be used to generate electricity. Hawaii has been conducting experiments since the 1970s, but 2020 is the earliest any OTEC system is likely to be working.

CASE STUDY

France: The Rance Barrage

A tidal range (difference between high and low tides) of 11.6 m makes the Rance Estuary an ideal coastal barrage site. Tides rise twice every 24 hours, moving at 20 km/h. At spring tide they are even higher. Water passes through several tunnels in the dam, each with blades that turn a turbine to generate power. As the tide turns and goes out, the blades reverse so electricity is still generated. The barrage is productive most of the time. Transport is not disrupted. Ships can move through a lock and, conveniently, the road built on top of the barrage cuts the journey round the estuary by 30 km.

Tidal power generation is not yet widespread, but the technology is not new. France developed its Rance barrage in 1966.

Geothermal Energy

Geothermal energy is heat energy that comes from deep within the Earth. Places that have this resource – usually areas where there are volcanoes, geysers and hot springs – are extremely lucky. Not only can tourism businesses take advantage of people wanting to see these natural features, but steam and heat from these sources can be used to generate electricity. Iceland, California, Italy, Japan and New Zealand are all volcanic areas that make use of this natural energy resource. Kenya, the Azores and several countries in Central America all have great potential.

Making Heat and Power

Heat deep in the Earth's core travels through the mantle as magma – melted rock. The Earth's crust is broken into pieces called plates, and at the edges of these plates magma comes very close to the surface so the heat can be used as an energy

Nicaragua has more geothermal energy potential than any other Central American country because it has a whole chain of volcanoes along its Pacific coast.

CASE STUDY

Iceland: The Blue Lagoon

The Blue Lagoon, a popular tourist destination, lies 40 minutes' drive south-west of Iceland's capital Reykjavik. This huge pool of mineral-rich, geothermally heated water is in the middle of a lava field. The Svartsengi geothermal power plant situated next to it pumps the water up from 2 km below the Earth. Minerals in the lagoon water are reputed to have significant health benefits. Skin conditions like psoriasis and eczema are often improved. Skincare products are made and sold at the Blue Lagoon, as well as being exported across the world.

People enjoy the heated waters of the Blue Lagoon in Iceland.

source. Water is pumped down a hole called an injection well. When it hits hot rocks beneath the surface some of it is turned into steam and some water is just heated by the rocks. Both steam and hot water rise back to the surface. These are separated for different uses. The steam is used to turn electricity-generating turbines, and the hot water is used to heat buildings and greenhouses. Geothermal energy can even be used to grow tropical bananas near the Arctic Circle!

Geothermal Energy and the Environment

No fuel is burned in a geothermal energy plant, so emissions of dangerous gases are almost zero. Compared with a traditional power plant, using fossil fuels such as oil as its source, a geothermal station produces between one and three per cent of the carbon-dioxide emissions and three per cent of the acid rain. One particular cause of acid rain, hydrogen sulphide, can be a problem as it is found

naturally in geothermal water, but there are now ways of cleaning hydrogen sulphide out of the water so it does not cause pollution. Any unused steam and water is injected back into the Earth so there is no waste. Geothermal energy is a practical, sustainable source of energy, and the only big problem with it is that it can only be harnessed in certain parts of the world.

TAKE ACTION

There are a number of ways of saving energy:
- Turn off lights when you leave a room.
- Cook in the microwave rather than the oven – it uses far less energy.
- Have a shower rather than a bath – it takes less energy to heat the water.
- Buy energy-efficient electrical appliances.
- Do not leave electrical equipment on standby – it uses almost as much power as when the device is turned on.

Nuclear Power

Nuclear power is a more sustainable form of power production than using oil because nuclear power requires very little of its raw material – uranium. Uranium is also found in many countries. Spent (used) fuel can be recycled, which increases its sustainability. However, the use of nuclear power has always been controversial, mainly because of the risk of radioactive leaks and questions over how to safely dispose of the spent fuel.

The Fuel – Uranium

The raw material used in nuclear power is uranium, a radioactive element found in tiny amounts in most rocks. It is only worth mining when there is a high concentration one place. It is also present in seawater and could be taken from there if prices were to increase enough to make this possible, giving it much greater potential.

Very little raw material is needed for nuclear energy – only 50 tonnes per year provides all the world's nuclear power stations. In contrast, 500 tonnes of coal are needed every hour for all coal-fired power stations globally. Uranium contains energy in a concentrated form, so the volume of fuel needed is much smaller, making transport and storage easier and cheaper than coal and oil.

How Nuclear Power Works

We get energy from uranium atoms by splitting them in a process known as nuclear fission.

An open-pit uranium mine in Australia. The damage to the landscape caused by uranium mining is one of the problems of nuclear power.

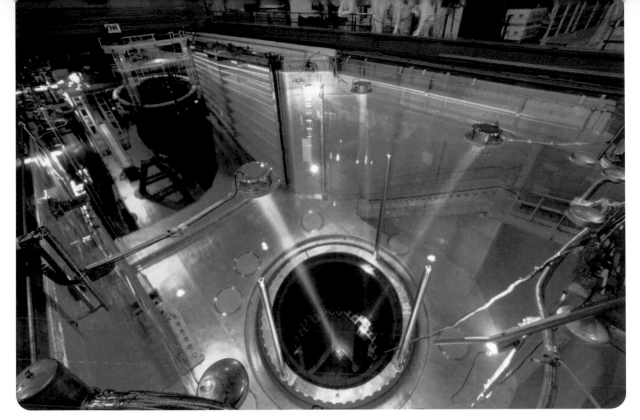

A reactor in a nuclear power plant in France. The reactors carefully control the chain reactions that take place in nuclear fission.

A particle called a neutron is fired at a uranium atom. This splits the atom, releasing energy as heat and radiation. More neutrons are also released as the atom splits. These then hit other uranium atoms, splitting them and continuing the process in a chain reaction. Because of this chain reaction, huge amounts of energy can be gained from quite a small amount of uranium.

Fission generates heat in a machine called a nuclear reactor in the same way as coal creates heat in a boiler. The heat is used to turn water into steam, which powers generators, creating electricity. Nuclear reactors control the chain reaction and also release heat in controlled amounts.

The Benefits of Nuclear Power

Nuclear-power generation produces low amounts of carbon dioxide, so it contributes little to global warming. It is considered an almost completely 'clean' power source. The technology is available, including ways of making the process safe. A single plant can generate a large amount of electricity.

Nuclear waste is transported to the nuclear energy site at Sellafield in the United Kingdom.

The Problems with Nuclear Power

At the moment, nuclear power is not truly
sustainable. Resources of uranium should last up
to about 2070. That is plenty to supply one or two
more generations of power stations, but just like
fossil fuels, uranium is a limited resource, so other
nuclear sources must be found if we want to
continue using fission to create usable energy.

The chain reaction takes place in the core of
the reactor and is controlled by the number of
fuel rods inserted or removed. Reactors are very
carefully monitored, but problems do occur. If a
malfunction is not fixed, it can lead to meltdown –
when the system overheats. In the worst situation
radiation can escape. Systems are built so they
do not explode, but in the past – with lower
levels of technology and safety precautions –
nuclear power-plant disasters occurred. In the
short term radiation leaks can cause serious health
problems for people, and these can continue over
time. Radioactive leaks can contaminate water
supplies and radiation can remain in the
atmosphere for years.

One of the biggest concerns of nuclear power is
how to safely dispose of the waste. At the moment,
it is buried in stockpiles deep underground, but this
is not a safe method. Radioactivity can leak from
the stockpiles and get into the air, affecting the
health of people and wildlife, and infecting the
ground and water supplies.

Nuclear Fusion

Many scientists agree that a process called nuclear
fusion could be the answer to safe nuclear energy.
In this process, the nuclei of the atoms are joined
together rather than split apart. This is a difficult

process to control and research is continuing, but if scientists can find a way of safely harnessing energy by nuclear fusion it has great potential. It releases less radioactivity than fission, and it could be almost everlasting because the nuclei of several different elements, including hydrogen and iron, could be used.

A Sustainable Future?

It is clear that we must manage our use of oil and its products in a more sustainable way, in order to reduce the harmful environmental impacts and preserve for as long as possible what is left of this valuable fossil fuel. Major steps have already been taken in making safer the extraction, transport and storage of oil. Many refineries are subject to high standards to control their emissions of polluting gases. There are a number of alternatives to oil as an energy source, and as technology develops, these will become real options for a sustainable future.

The choices made by individuals can have great power in influencing decisions made by oil companies and governments, so the most important element of sustainable development is for everyone to play their part.

CASE STUDY

Japan: Nuclear Emergency

In September 1999, Japan had a nuclear emergency caused by a major uranium leak. Radiation levels at the Tokaimura nuclear reprocessing plant reached 15,000 times higher than normal. Hundreds of people living close to the plant had to leave their homes. A 6-km 'forbidden zone' was set up around the plant. An even worse incident had occurred at Tokaimura two years earlier, in 1997, when 35 workers were contaminated after a fire and an explosion led to a radiation leak.

Emergency workers keep people away from the Tokaimura plant after a radiation leak.

Facts and Figures

Top Five Countries with the Most Oil Reserves (2007)

Country	Million barrels
Saudi Arabia	262,400
Iran	138,400
Iraq	115,000
Kuwait	101,500
Venezuela	87,000

Top Five Countries with the Most Natural Gas Reserves (2007)

Country	Trillion cubic metres
Russia	44.65
Iran	27.80
Qatar	25.60
United States	5.98
Nigeria	5.30

Top Five Oil-Producing Countries (2007)

Country	Barrels per day
Saudi Arabia	10,413,000
Russia	9,978,000
United States	6,879,000
Iran	4,401,000
China	3,743,000

Top Five Natural Gas-Producing Countries (2007)

Country	Million tonnes of oil equivalent
Russia	546.7
United States	499.4
Canada	165.3
Iran	100.7
Norway	80.7

Top Five Oil-Consuming Countries (2007)

Country	Barrels per day
United States	20,698,000
China	7,855,000
Japan	5,051,000
India	2,748,000
Russia	2,699,000

Top Five Natural-Gas Consuming Countries (2007)

Country	Billion cubic metres
United States	652.9
Russia	438.8
Iran	111.8
Canada	94.0
United Kingdom	91.4

Source: BP Statistical Review of World Energy, 2008

Further Resources

Websites

http://science.howstuffworks.com/oil-refining4.htm
Details on oil refining, with diagrams of the processes.

http://www.eia.doe.gov/kids/energyfacts/sources/
non-renewable/oil.html
Information on oil refining as well as oil products
and uses.

http://www.naturalgas.org
Lots of detail on many aspects of natural-gas
exploration and production.

http://www.eia.doe.gov/kids/energyfacts/sources/
renewable/wind.html
How wind energy works, production methods and
environmental impacts.

http://www.tvakids.com/electricity/nuclear.htm
Information about nuclear power.

http://www.bbc.co.uk/climate/adaptation/nuclear_
power.shtml
Nuclear power and climate change.

http://news.bbc.co.uk/1/hi/sci/tech/6616651.stm
How a solar power station works.

http://iceland.ednet.ns.ca/schedule.htm
Facts about geothermal power in Iceland.

http://www.sahel.org.uk/photogallery.htm
Photos of biomass collection in Africa.

http://www.wasteonline.org.uk/resources/Information
Sheets/Plastics.htm
A broad range of recycling plastics information.

http://www.tvakids.com/electricity/hydro.htm
How hydroelectric power works.

http://www.solar.coppe.ufrj.br/itaipu.html
Information on the Itaipu dam project.

Books

Leacock, Elspeth, *The Exxon Valdez Oil Spill*
(Environmental Disasters), Facts on File, 2005

Morgan, Sally, *Oil, Gas and Coal, Pros and Cons of
Energy* (Energy Debate), Wayland, 2007

Morris, Neil, *Fossil Fuels* (Energy Sources), Franklin
Watts, 2006

Oxlade, Chris, *Energy Technology* (New Technology),
Evans Publishing, 2008

Oxlade, Chris, *How We Use Oil* (Using Materials),
Raintree, 2004

Ravilious, Kate, *Power* (Dilemmas in Modern Science),
Evans Publishing, 2008

Snedden, Robert, *Energy from Fossil Fuels* (Essential
Energy), Heinemann Library, 2007

Stringer, John, *Energy* (Sustainable Futures), Evans
Publishing, 2005

Glossary

barrage a barrier or dam built across an estuary to harness tidal energy.

biodegradable something that breaks down naturally when it comes into contact with micro-organisms in the earth and air.

biofuels fuels that come from decaying organic matter that has recently died, as opposed to fossil fuels, which come from matter that died millions of years ago.

biomass decaying organic matter used to create biofuels. Biomass can be crops and plants, but it can also be animal waste.

chain reaction a chemical reaction, which, once started, continues under its own energy. One reaction leads to the next, and so on, until deliberately stopped.

climate change a change in global temperatures that can result in extreme weather conditions. Climate change can happen naturally, but human activities are increasing the rate of this change.

crude oil oil in its natural state, as it is pumped out of the ground, before it is refined.

distillation a method of heating crude oil so it is split up into its different parts.

economy the supply of money gained by a community or country from goods and services.

ecosystem all the plants and animals in an area, along with their environment.

exploitation the use of natural resources in a way that harms the environment or local people.

fossil fuels energy resources formed by dead organic matter, which becomes compacted through heat and pressure. Coal, oil and natural gas are all fossil fuels.

fuel rods sticks of concentrated nuclear fuel, which can be inserted into or taken out of a nuclear reactor to affect the speed and scale of the process.

geology the study of the Earth, its structure and natural features such as rocks.

global warming the process by which temperatures across the world are increasing. Global warming does happen naturally, but some temperature increase is caused by human activity such as burning fossil fuels in cars and industry. Such activity releases greenhouse gases into the atmosphere.

greenhouse gas a gas that can cause global warming – the heating up of the Earth's atmosphere. Carbon dioxide and methane are examples of greenhouse gases.

habitat a place where a plant or animal lives.

infrastructure the assets a country has that help support its economy, such as water supply, road systems and power supplies.

insolation heat energy from the Sun. The name comes from the words 'incoming solar radiation'.

LEDC less economically developed country – one of the poorer countries of the world. LEDCs include all of Africa, Asia (except Japan), Latin America and the Caribbean, and Melanesia, Micronesia and Polynesia.

LNG liquefied natural gas. Natural gas travels more efficiently and cheaply as a liquid because it has more energy per unit volume.

magma liquid rock that exists in the mantle of the Earth. It can reach up to the crust and sometimes bursts through as volcanic eruptions.

MEDC more economically developed country – one of the richer countries of the world. MEDCs include the whole of Europe, North America, Australia, New Zealand and Japan.

methane a gas that forms the main ingredient of natural gas found in the ground. Methane is a greenhouse gas that contributes to climate change.

oil shale surface deposits of oil mixed with sand, silt and soft rocks like shale.

petroleum another word for oil.

photodegradable something that breaks down naturally when it comes into contact with sunlight.

plastics synthetic products, made from polymers, but which may contain other substances. The raw material of most plastics today is petroleum, but organically based plastics do exist.

pollution harmful substances in the environment, often present as a result of human activity.

polymer a long chain of hydrocarbon molecules, used to make plastics. Polymers can occur naturally or be man-made.

radioactivity the emission of radiation or particles from the breakdown of atomic nuclei, such as uranium.

rainforest forest that grows in an area that is very hot and that has high rainfall all year. Rainforests can support more types of plants and animals than any other ecosystem.

recycling the process by which materials are collected and used again as 'raw' materials for new products.

refinery a factory where raw materials, such as crude oil, are purified.

renewable energy energy generated from sources that can be replaced or renewed, such as the wind or the Sun.

reserves the amount of something like oil or coal that a country has left to be exploited.

seismic exploration the use of seismic waves to explore structures underground, usually when searching for new oil or natural-gas resources.

smog a mixture of fog and smoke, forming an air pollutant.

sustainability a form of development that benefits a country or community's economy, but also benefits the local environment and the quality of life of its inhabitants.

tundra treeless areas found at high altitudes and the Arctic, where the subsoil is always frozen.

wind turbine a modern version of a windmill. It consists of a tall tower with two or three blades. The blades move in the wind and the system can generate electrical energy.

Index